WORDS
ARE YOUR
SUPER POWER

BY

A.S. STEPHENS

CONTENTS

Introduction 5

Chapter 1: Alter Egos – Taking Inventory of Who You Are and Where You Are Now 9

Chapter 2: Superheroes – How You Choose to Fight Your Battles 25

Chapter 3: Villains – The Words that Destroy and Suck Power from Your Life 37

Chapter 4: Superpowers – The Strengths That Words Hide or Reveal 51

Chapter 5: Plan of Attack 65

Chapter 6: Training Plan – Conditioning Yourself for Success 73

Chapter 7: Your Authentic Self 83

Conclusion 89

INTRODUCTION

You are a superhero. You wake up every day and move through life, facing many battles and achieving small victories with each challenge you overcome. But are there days you don't feel like this is true? Are there days when the words of people seem to sap all the power from you?

In this book, you'll learn how to take inventory of who and where you are right now, the words that destroy and suck power from your life, and the words that help you fight your battles. You'll also be able to identify the best words for each battle you face and condition yourself to live successfully, confidently, and authentically in your new identity as a superhero.

My goal is to help you understand the principles behind the power of words and give you practical tips that will help. To let you know that you are not alone and help you formulate an action plan so your life can change. To help you identify the source of the negative words and tips on how to begin to switch them out for positive ones. My goal is to give you tools so that you can live a happier life with words of support and encouragement in your head. To let you know that when you try something new, no matter the outcome, there are positive words and affirmation you can tell yourself so you can keep trying until you find the things that work for your life.

Let me tell you a little bit about myself. I grew up content with some areas of my life, like family, religion, and books, and unsettled in others, like anything requiring hand-eye coordination and speaking in front of more than five people. From the age of around 20, I would often face times of frustration and sadness, without ever really knowing why. I knew that I could be living a better life but was unsure how to go about it without destroying what I loved about my life, my relationships with family and friends, the love of learning new things, an interesting and tiring job with great people just to name a few. Words had something to do with it. I was sure of this because I would fight the tapes of negative words playing through my mind. So, I figured if I could change the words playing through my mind, I could change my life. On the other hand, I was wary. I didn't want everything to change.

I loved being able to entertain myself, the stories running through my head. My mind is an active and imaginative place. I didn't hate my job, but I wanted to try something new and to work towards being the best version of myself instead of settling for what I could get. So, I started learning about words and how to use them to change my life. Along the way, I discovered the power in words, those spoken to me and those I spoke to myself. I began to learn how to change the words I spoke to myself and in doing so, I changed my life.

It didn't happen overnight. It took almost six months before I started to recognize I felt different going through my days. Words in books had always fascinated me. Throughout the process of changing my life, the words I said to myself began to do the same. Instead of feeling beat up by my words, I began to feel encouraged. My first thought when trying something new was no longer "You'll fail." It became "Let's see what happens." My first reaction to making a mistake was no longer, "You're so stupid." Instead, it changed to "What did you learn and what can you do better?". These changes in words profoundly changed how I saw myself, how I showed up each day, and even how I felt about myself.

One day, during my time of prayer and reflection, I felt the call to help others who may be struggling as I was. To help the person who lives each day in conflict, battling the tapes of negative words playing through their head. To help the person who gives themselves a daily pep talk, even if they struggle to believe it. I wanted to help them understand the process of switching out the negative words for positive words. I wanted to give them a chance to not be mentally exhausted at the end of the day, a chance to have some of the sadness go away and the frustrations leave with it. Maybe I could help someone so their smile could be real, or their breaths could be easy.

Are you such a person? Do you feel like some battles are harder than they should be? Do you end more days feeling tired and defeated than triumphant? Do you often feel like life wins and you lose?

If so, there may be villains sneaking up on you but only because you have neglected to put your unique superpower to use. Words, spoken internally and externally, are the superpowers that can help you turn your defeats into triumphs. Ask yourself, what words make up your unique superpower?

This book is a practical guide for you to work through and discover your individual superpower. I will share stories of how I identified my own, but I cannot tell you what yours are.

Your superpowers are unique to you and you must do the work to discover them for yourself. If you are looking for someone to give you the answers, this book is not for you. If you need to know where to start and how to make progress in your life, this book can help.

Are you ready to begin to change the words you speak so you can change your life and thrive?

CHAPTER 1:

ALTER EGOS –
TAKING INVENTORY OF WHO YOU ARE AND WHERE YOU ARE NOW

A pair of glasses can change the way people perceive you. Don't believe me? Just ask Clark Kent. With his glasses on, he becomes a mild-mannered employee of *The Daily Planet*, a metropolitan newspaper. When the glasses come off, his clothes are changed and he wears a cape, he becomes a different person. He can leap tall buildings in a single bound, he's faster than a speeding bullet and more powerful than a locomotive. When he flies, people look up in the sky and mistake him for a bird or a plane. Then they realize, nope it's Superman.

A mask can hide your identity. Need proof? Ask Bruce Wayne. He's just your ordinary, everyday billionaire living the playboy lifestyle. Until the bat signal lights up the sky. He puts on his mask and cloak, arms his belt with gadgets and weapons, and calls his Batmobile developed from the imaginations of engineers, and fights crime in the city of Gotham. In an instant, he's Batman.

A suit can give you anonymity when others knowing who you are will set you up to be mocked. Have questions? Interview

Peter Parker. His whole life changed once he was bitten by a radioactive spider. To add insult to injury, it was while he was in high school doing his best to fit in. But he acquired the power to climb walls and hang from ceilings without equipment. Is it any wonder that he dons a red and blue suit to help others as Spiderman?

Sometimes, you are simply born or sculpted into a community that shelters and teaches you to stand in your own power. Need insight? Princess Diana of Themyscira can give you some. She uses her strength to fight for the right to return a lost officer home and battle crime in a world not her own. The new world around her was unprepared for her greatness. The only name that made enough sense was Wonder Woman.

So, who are you? Were you born with a power cultivated and nurtured to reach its full potential? Maybe you were born with abilities that seemed out of this world and taught to hide them because people wouldn't understand. Every day, putting on your glasses to remind yourself that you need to hide who you were born to be.

Were you born as an ordinary person and life happened to make you extraordinary in a time when you were unprepared? As a result, you spend your time doing good behind a mask because you are convinced no one can accept the real you without attempting to harm those in your life.

Were you born into privilege and faced with early tragedy causing your perspective on life to change? Now you use that privilege for good, balancing your actions, so you don't embarrass the family that you love?

Taking Inventory of Who You Are and Where You Are Now

Who are you?

When we are born, we are identified by sex. "It's a boy" or "It's a girl" are words spoken by the doctor, depending on the biological makeup of our genes. But afterwards, life is unpredictable. It's a story based on the characters who are in it. These characters include your biological parents or the people who raised you—your providers in the early years of your life.

Think about this:

- How was the environment you were raised in?
- How were you treated?
- Did you receive love and kindness along with words of affirmation and praise?
- Or were you seen as a burden and told you were stupid, no good, and worthless?

The words spoken around you and about you are the beginning of the tapes that play back in your mind. These are the words integrated into your personality and often the words you tell yourself subconsciously throughout life. They guide your daily interactions and influence decisions.

In addition to the words that you heard, there were the actions you saw.

- What actions did you witness as you were learning to process the world around you?
- As you recognized sounds and learned to read, what words did you tell yourself about these actions?
- If you grew up in a spiritual household, did you tell yourself that prayer was a requirement before every meal or before going to bed every night?

- If you grew up in a household where one parent was an alcoholic, did you tell yourself that after your parent had a couple of drinks it was better for you to be quiet or hide away so you couldn't be found?

The words that you applied to the actions around you are just as important as the words that you heard. Perhaps you felt that when words and actions matched, life became a little easier. But what happened when words and actions did not match? How did you learn which one to believe?

This conflict inside you surely produced other perceptions and words, as well as many questions. Unasked or unanswered questions leave a void that needs to be filled. So, what words filled the void in your life? Once those words are accepted, the brain looks for reasons to reinforce the answers and they become a part of your reality.

Additionally, there are feelings and emotions. How were you taught to respond to pain and hurt feelings? Think about the first time that someone told you something negative about yourself. Did you tell anyone? How did they respond? Think about the person who spoke the negative words. Was it someone you trusted? Did you believe them? Do you hold the same belief today?

When negative words find someplace to live inside of you, there is usually already a foundation of negativity. Identifying the place where the negative words latch on can give you an idea of the origin of the alter ego operating in your life. This is also true of positive words. When someone tells you something positive, these words also look for a place to live. Unfortunately, most people have heard more negativity than positivity in their life. This means there are more places for negative words to attach and live. Because of this, the negative words always seem to outweigh the positive.

How do you react to people in authority? Were you taught they were right based simply on the position they held? Words spoken to you by people of authority in your life tend to hold more weight. Can you identify the heaviest words spoken in your life?

Think about the people you've come across who hold the most authority.

- How did they contribute to your alter ego?
- What words do you still live your life by today?
- Are there words you can accept, understand, and process that help you face hard times or the nightmarish situations in your life?

The answers to these questions and the situations that come to mind all form the basis of your alter ego. They inform how you present yourself to the world. If you are taught not to show weakness, you focus on showing up as strong, needing no one to help you. You don't cry because tears are for the weak and you pretend to have it all together. In truth, you live by the motto, fake it until you make it. Think of the people that you identify with the most. Do you like them because they never make a mistake? If they work within a team, do you consider them weak for not being able to handle everything on their own?

As a kid, were you told "there isn't such a thing as a stupid question?" This is a nice saying, until you asked the same question more than once (trying to get an understanding), and were told, "you should know ... the answer was just given to you." Now, in your quest for learning, do you freely ask questions? Or do you still censor the questions you ask to avoid other people becoming frustrated with you. Are you left with the impression that observing something being done correctly automatically means you should know how to do it yourself? Even if you were never directly taught?

How would you identify your alter ego? There are many ways. You can instinctively know your alter ego, or it may be so engrained in you that you have to dig deeper to find the origin. Additionally, different aspects of your alter ego can be formed at different times in your life.

Let me tell you the story about the creation of one part of my alter ego. I was born smart. It has taken me time to realize this is not a statement of arrogance but simply fact. I believe that everyone is born smart in some capacity. It is only after our introduction to society that specific areas of intelligence are considered valuable. These areas usually consist of things like math or science skills. At the same time, other areas are considered basically worthless, take for instance drawing.

I was born with the ability to observe things around me and to understand them quickly. Observation was a skill for me, and I observed best and learned most from a place of safety. My parents tell stories of how I wouldn't go to very many people unless they had food. Even in family gatherings, I would follow the food and when the food was gone, so was I. I preferred to be around people that I knew well and saw often.

Taking Inventory of Who You Are and Where You Are Now

Observing my older sisters and other kids, I also learned to crawl earlier than average kids, and I learned to read quickly. It was in books that I found a haven. They became a place of fantasy and refuge. Words are serious business, but the ongoing love of words can have a side effect. Words spoken to me, especially negative words, I considered as truth and had a profound impact on my life. My first experience with negative words being spoken about me, that I remember clearly, happened in third grade. It was in mathematics class to be exact, one of my favorite subjects.

I was a part of the talented and gifted group, TAG, and I was in an advanced mathematics class. In essence, I was placed with other smart kids to be challenged with more difficult criteria—this was so that we wouldn't get bored in class or fall asleep or start causing trouble. Advanced mathematics moved at a faster place. On this particular day, the class schedule was different, so I was in the regular mathematics class. The teacher put problems up on the board and students were chosen to go up and solve the problem. It seemed that writing on the board in third grade is every kid's dream. Except me.

It was an interesting time for a couple of reasons: first, I was looking at problems that we had already advanced beyond; second, I could tell the teacher was going to call on me, and I didn't want her to. But I did not get what I wanted. My name was called to solve the most difficult subtraction problem. I don't remember the exact problem, but I do remember the top number ended in three zeros. Let's just say the number was 5,000. Reluctantly, I proceeded to solve the subtraction problem as I was taught, crossing out 500 and making it 499, so that I could make the last zero into a 10 to proceed.

As soon as I finished adjusting the top number, the teacher reacted as though I was attempting to change the laws of mathematics. "Wrong!" She called out from the back of the class. "You can't do that. It is not how you solve the problem."

I could feel my face grow hot as embarrassment rose within me. Not only was the teacher loud, but now everyone was looking at me, and I could see some smirks. I responded as calmly as I could. "I'm not finished yet, Ms. …"

"Well, your first step is wrong."

"This is the way we were taught," I said. As this point, I wanted to disappear from the room and never come back. Unfortunately, Ms. Franklin was also my homeroom teacher. There was nowhere I could go.

Ms. Franklin walked up to the board and told me to sit down. Telling the class that you can't borrow from zero, she proceeded to solve the problem in what I considered the long way. As if I had not been embarrassed enough, she added commentary as she was working out the problem for the class.

"I don't know what they are teaching in that so called smart class, but this is why everyone should be in the same class. Kids go around thinking they're smart and can't even solve a basic math problem."

To say I was humiliated is an understatement. It took everything inside of me not to let the tears pricking at my eyes fall. On top of it all, I still didn't see the fundamental difference in our approaches to solve the problem—because she got the same answer that was on my paper. But her words stuck with me and an aspect of my alter ego was formed out of the words forming in my mind. "Don't let people see how smart you are. They will only humiliate and embarrass you. Do your work and hide the process as often as possible. Only show the end result. They can't make fun of something they can't see."

This narrative informed my view of life for a long time. Throughout the majority of my schooling, I would turn in papers without the process explained. Especially in math, I did all work on a separate piece of paper, only handing in the answer. Instructions stating, "show your work" were the bane of my existence, until I learned I could write the operations of the problem out separately with the answer to get full credit.

It was not until college that I began to see a different perspective. After a variety of changes, I decided to major in mathematics education. One professor told me "having children show their work will let you know if there is a mathematical or a conceptual error. You become better at explaining concepts when you see how it translates in their mind." This made sense to me.

Those words, over 13 years after the initial event, stuck in my mind and began to chip at the wall of words that had become an alter ego in my life. I was smart, but it was not okay to show it. Maybe hiding it didn't help either?

Now, it's your turn to identify the alter egos in your life.

Exercise: Finding your Alter Egos

How do you know where your current state is?

Take inventory of your life. Write out the areas in your life which you are happiest.

....
....
....
....
....
....
....
....
....

What about these areas make you happy?

....
....
....
....
....
....
....
....
....

Taking Inventory of Who You Are and Where You Are Now

What actions do you take every day to work towards maintaining or improving your happiness in these areas?

....

....

....

....

....

....

....

....

....

What words came to your mind as you were thinking about these areas and the actions you take? Jot them down here. Be completely honest with yourself, no one else has to read this.

....

....

....

....

....

....

....

....

....

Which areas in your life are you not happy with or want to see improvement in? Write them here.

....
....
....
....
....
....
....
....
....

What don't you like about these areas in your life? Make a list.

....
....
....
....
....
....
....
....
....
....
....

Write out any words or thoughts that came to mind when you were writing. Be honest with yourself.

....
....
....
....
....
....
....
....

Reflect on your experience in making the lists of positive areas and improvement areas in your life. What past experiences or stories came to mind? What words did you hear in your mind that made writing the lists easier or more challenging? Was there anything that you hesitated to write down? Include it here.

....
....
....
....
....
....
....
....

Read the lists, thoughts, and words you wrote during this exercise out loud to yourself. During your read through, did anything else come to mind? Did new words come to mind? Did any memories come up? Write them down.

....
....
....
....
....
....
....

Separate the words, thoughts, and memories into a positive reaction list and a negative reaction lists, based off how they affected you. This will help identity the words pushing you forward and the words holding you back. There may be times where words seemed positive but caused a negative reaction in you and vice versa. It's important to identify both the words and your reactions to them. Using words that cause a negative reaction is counterproductive, regardless of how positive they appear to be.

....
....
....
....
....
....
....

Taking Inventory of Who You Are and Where You Are Now

What aspects of your alter ego can you identify and when did they begin?

....
....
....
....
....
....
....

Finally, write down the aspects of the life you want to live. What job or career do you want to have? Where do you want to live? What legacy do you want to leave, etc.? Include the words that come up as you are thinking about each aspect. This list will be used for another exercise later in the book. It's okay if you cannot think of everything right now. These lists can be added to as other words or memories come to mind. Right now, you're looking for a starting point to work from.

....
....
....
....
....
....
....
....

Now, you have an idea of the alter egos that have developed in your life along with where they came from. Notice how words have affected or currently affect you and the influence they continue to have in your life. Think about the words pushing you forward as well as the ones holding you back. Next, we'll look at how you've chosen to fight battles in your past.

CHAPTER 2:

SUPERHEROES –
HOW YOU CHOOSE TO FIGHT YOUR BATTLES

My favorite superhero of all time is Wonder Woman. She is not a woman in distress, even when she gets tied up by her opponents. Wonder Woman can get herself out of situations with a lasso of truth and her bracelets. I like her because she's a strong Amazonian woman with a group of loving women behind her. She is fantastic.

Princess Diana of Themyscira was raised by group of women who taught her to appreciate herself and the history of her country. To top it all off, she's a princess who made the choice to help others. She fought to be able to return a stranded man to his world and chose to leave her safe environment to go into a world at war. Princess Diana gave up her guaranteed rule and place of ownership to enter the unknown. The way I see it, she was born a princess and raised a hero.

Next is Superman. He is a foreigner to our planet, an alien who was sent here so he could have a chance at a better life. The change in environment and constant exposure to the sun changed his biological makeup. He gained more power because of it. He can run faster and jump higher. Raised by loving parents in the country, his powers make him stand out, whereas on his home planet he would be ordinary. He knows love from his adoptive parents, the value of sacrifice from his birth parents, and is shown through example how to model both to the world.

Afterward, Clark Kent chose to make a difference and use the gifts he was born with to help the world at large. When he isn't "saving the world," he makes his living at *The Daily Planet*, a place known for using words to inform and challenge the world. He was born a hero.

Then, there is Spiderman. To be honest, Spiderman is one of the heroes who kind of creeps me out. It's no fault of his own. It's entirely because of how he contracted his powers. He was bit by a spider. As if that's not bad enough, he was bit by an experimental radioactive spider with the ability to change his very DNA so he can do spiderlike things. Can you imagine? *Yeah, let me go hang on a wall and shoot webs from my wrists.*

I am not a huge fan of arachnids. That said, I cannot deny that once Peter Parker figured out what was going on and made the choice to help his city become safer, he displayed both strength and an effective use of his powers. "With great power comes great responsibility." This phase, told to him by his Uncle Ben, plays on repeat in his mind. The power of those words awoke something in Peter Parker, and they helped him decide to use his powers for good. They evoked an emotion so strong he made a decision that changed the trajectory of his life. Like Wonder Woman and Superman, he made a choice to help. Unlike them, he was not born into a position of power, nor was he born a superhero—he become one through an accident.

And we dare not forget about Iron Man, the genius billionaire targeted for death who escaped using the help of a fellow prisoner and his brain. He built an arc reactor so that he could live and a metal suit to fight his way out. It was an act of technological brilliance. He went on to create a better suit, donning it on a regular basis to take out those who had wronged him. Throughout the process, he had to deal with the mental, physical, and psychological issues arising from his kidnapping and the betrayal of a family friend.

Tony Stark changed his company and his life to fight not only crime, but also against threats to society. His family life, while financially stable, doesn't come across as nurturing. He used the resources left to him to build something greater. He became a superhero not by birth, not from his environment, nor even by accident. He was a self-made one.

People find themselves in similar situations today. Some are born into a world of words and taught how to use them. They grow up surrounded by people who love and support them. Their gifts and talents are recognized, and they are raised learning how to use them appropriately. They are born into families where they are wanted, adored, and cherished. Each day they were encouraged to go farther, be stronger, and to do their best. This group of people grew up with positive words around them with an underlying support showing them they were loved exactly as they are. They were trained in the appreciation of who they are, their history, their culture and taught how to wield their talents and gifts to the greatest benefit. They know their value, importance, and worth. Others look at them and think they have an intuitive understanding of the power of words. Like Princess Diana of Themyscira, these people make the choice to use what they know, leave their safe zone, and help others.

Another group of people are born into a different environment. They are brought up around negativity and taunting. These people grew up being picked on and bullied. They had to live in a house with various kinds of abuse and wanted a way out. One day, these people who are used to abuse and negativity hear a compliment. They are praised for something they do or an aspect of their character. They hear positive words that begin to penetrate the layers of negativity in their life. Something changes. These words may come from a workshop, an overheard conversation, a teacher, a book, a movie, or a television show. It is not the source that makes a difference, it is the words that spark a reaction deep inside of them. At the time, it seems like an accident. A series of coincidences colliding in a perfect moment resulting in a perspective change. Their understanding of the power of words is not intuitive, it is learned later in life. Once they understand, they cannot go back to the way they were before. They follow the words of Uncle Ben, "With great power comes great responsibility." With a new understanding of the power they hold, they choose to use it responsibly.

Let's not forget about the group of people that seem to have it all. From the outside looking in, they exude wealth, power, love, support, connections, and anything else they could possibly need to be successful in life. Yet on the inside, something is missing. If asked, these people would not be able to articulate, but they just know that something isn't quite right. They go through the motions of living, incomplete until tragedy strikes. They are imprisoned and left to die. It may be a physical prison, a mental one, a psychological one, or a combination of them all.

These types of people are stuck. They face their own mortality in pain, mourning a betrayal, the loss of a loved one, or any situation that seems hopeless. The individuals in this group may start to question if living is worth the battle. At the moment when all hope is lost, someone comes along to lend a helping hand. The actual event: an act of kindness, a conversation, a smile, an acknowledgement of their pain, a hug, is secondary to the reaction inside of them. They begin to hope again, to believe they are not alone and that they can make it through.

Through this act, whatever it may be, they gain strength to continue living. A temporary fix is assembled so getting out of bed is possible. With the help of a trusted individual, they begin to fight for freedom and on the other side of the tragedy they begin to wonder how they endured. They use their own reflections on who and what helped. Making a choice to live differently, they begin to dismantle the temporary fix and create something better, raising the standard. They make the choice to intentionally dig into the power of words and, like Tony Stark, become self-made.

Using everything they have learned this group helps others who are going through situations like the one they came out of. Their goal is to help empower others, so their fight isn't as long, as hard or at the very least help them be more prepared.

The last group of people seem to have supernatural powers. Often, these individuals don't seem to be of this world. Everything about them is different. They live as outliers in their environments. Their talents are clear and natural, whether it be with words, writing, or any task they achieve simply and efficiently. Things get done quicker, words sound better, writing is more eloquent if they do it. These are the people who withstand criticisms with a smile, leap over negativity, face the obstacles and pressures of life knowing they will endure and win. They stand out while hidden behind a façade strong enough to allow them to fight behind the scenes without weakening their identity. They use specific words to fight, wielding them subtly.

This group works in the background, shining light on those around them, content with living in the shadows. They step forward briefly when needed only to fade back as soon as possible. They don't want the spotlight and prefer to live quietly and help others from their own corner of the world. They have learned to love themselves through the actions of those who raised them. They have learned to true sacrifice from role models in their life and use this knowledge to serve others. They are born heroes and like Clark Kent, content to live as a layperson.

Like each of these superheroes, *you* were born with gifts and talents into an environment which shaped your outlook on life. So, which are you? Were you born a superhero, raised and nurtured in your strengths and abilities? Or did you find out about them later in life? Were you "bitten" by a radioactive word spider that changed your DNA? Were you living out your life and one day a tragedy hit? As a result, you learned to fight, bringing out a brilliance in yourself you didn't know was there? Are you self-made, making a choice to help those connected to you, your community, city, country, or the world? Are you the quiet hero, knowing your strengths and willing to help, but content to live in the background helping others shine? Or are you a combination of them all?

It took a while for me to figure out that I don't have the all the qualities of one superhero. I have a combination of qualities with one or two coming from each of them. As far back as I can remember, words have fascinated me. I grew up reading and even though I didn't understand the true power of words at first, I knew they made the most brilliant pictures in my mind. Stories were best, but I would read anything I could get my hands on. Books, TV captions, cereal boxes—if it had words, I was going to read it. I loved that words could teach me more about the world around me. I even carried around a dictionary to help me when I didn't know what a word meant. It was like hitting the jackpot. The more I read, the more words I knew and the more words I knew, the bigger books I could read. It was a heavenly cycle.

. My mom raised me with an appreciation of books, being a reader herself, so I was raised understanding they were important. In the sixth grade, I began to write. I wanted to use a combination of words to create images for the reader. I was best with poetry, finding words to fit the rhyme and rhythm of a poem was like a game to me. It took time to learn what worked best for me. Princess Diana started as a young child, Peter Parker was a teenager, and Tony Stark was an adult. You can start to learn about your superpower at any age.

But, as I learned in school, words could also be used against me. I was bullied as a smart child who always read and needed glasses. My dad taught me to defend myself against physical harm, but kids can use words to cut and bruise. Physical bullying leaves bruises others can see, words leave bruises that damage from the inside. I needed to learn how to heal the internal wounds that were left behind. "Sticks and stones may break my bones, but words will never hurt me." This mantra was not entirely true, but it helped set me up to use words in fighting my battles. The more I said it to myself, the easier it was to believe. More importantly, it helped me to not show a reaction to others, so the bullying decreased.

In third grade, my family moved to Germany. This was my chance to start over in a new country. In Germany, I learned that words can actually sound different (foreign) but mean, basically, the same thing. I also learned that words did not have to be perfect, sometimes an approximation was good enough as long as I got my point across. It was at this time I began to understand that I preferred being left out of the spotlight, but I loved being able to use words to help others out. The importance of the using the right words started to matter, now I just needed to learn: How could I use the right words for a specific situation?

Ultimately, the type of superhero you are is secondary to the choosing to be one in the first place. Within the choice, the most important factor is being true to who you are. Will you be one who chooses to help the world, your country, your city, your community, or your family? All types are needed. Where do you fall and how will you show up?

Exercise

Make a list of all the major events in your life that had an impact on the person you are today.

....
....
....
....
....
....
....
....
....
....

What words did you hear during each event?

....
....
....
....
....
....
....
....
....
....

Who helped you? What did you learn about yourself?

What did you push away to deal with later?

How do you choose to face the world daily? What words help you?

Looking back on the major events in your life and how you face the world today, what misconceptions have you been living by?

What is the truth of each event?

How can you show up daily, based off these truths?

Most of how you show up today depends on events and words in your past. You cannot change the events, nor can you change the words that were spoken to you. However, you can change how you react going forward. Next, we'll take a look at the reaction words can have in your life.

CHAPTER 3:

VILLAINS – THE WORDS THAT DESTROY AND SUCK POWER FROM YOUR LIFE

Lex Luthor was the ultimate villain. He was rich, smart, and he had everything going for him. But there was an annoyance in his life: Superman. Lex Luthor would do anything to destroy Superman. He searched for the faintest weakness in the Man of Steel, and he found it in Kryptonite. A piece of his home planet that would counteract the strength that he gained from the sun and render Superman immobile, or at least weak enough to be injured.

Superman was also smart, but he had a soft spot for a certain reporter. Lois Lane. She was Luthor's way in. He would put Lois Lane in danger and when Superman was distracted, he could begin his main plan of destruction. Lex Luthor may not have been the strongest villain physically, but he was good at detecting weaknesses and exploiting them.

The Green Goblin was Spiderman's nemesis. The father of his best friend, who used his company to create and destroy. A genius in his own right, who wanted more than what he had. To accomplish this goal, he used the technology around him to make himself seem larger than life. He could not think of everything on his own, so he used the ideas and inventions of those around him to enhance the craziness of his mind for the purposes of bringing destruction.

When it comes Batman and the villains he faced, the Joker will forever live on in my mind as the most diabolical of the lot. The way that his mind worked was an act of brilliance filtered through the lens of apparent insanity. His plans exploited the worse side of people, the greed, jealousy, selfishness, etc. and he used these traits to create havoc.

Wonder Woman began her fight against Ares. The God of War. She fought with an immortal whose purpose was to exploit the deepest secrets, sorrows, hurts, and pains of others in such a way that violence was the result. Ares worked with thoughts and manipulated emotions to bring out the worst depravity of mankind.

Words make excellent villains. They can cut to the core of your identity. They can search out weaknesses, uncover secrets, and bring depravities to life. Words can be used to exploit, command, or destroy. There is an insidious power to words because even the ones that seem positive can be used to destroy. People can wield them with charisma and cause chaos. Alone, words can seem innocuous, but in the hands of the wrong person at the right time they can decimate and destroy.

The truth is: words can start wars and even kill. In the hands of a master manipulator, they can drain life and goodness from you so slowly that you don't recognize what they are doing until the weakness of death sets in.

- "You are so stupid; can't you do anything right?"
- "You'll never amount to anything."

- "You're just trailer trash."
- "You ugly cuss, I didn't want you anyways."
- "I wish you have never been born."
- "The world would have been better off if you weren't in it."
- "You're such a disappointment."
- "I'll never understand how someone so smart can act so dumb"
- "What's wrong with you?"
- "You never finish anything."
- "Can't you get anything right?"
- "I wish you were dead."

Villains. The words that work to destroy our lives, our hopes, and our dreams. The words that bring to light our deepest fears and insecurities. The words that can reduce us to nothing and hold us back from reaching for more. These are the negative words that lurk in the shadows, waiting for the right moment to attack. They are the words of doubt coming to us in our weakest moments seeking to destroy, the words hiding behind every success telling us we got lucky and it won't be long until our luck runs out.

In the life of every superhero, there lies a villain that needs to be fought. The villains are the words that stand opposite of you in every battle. Superman had Lex Luthor, Wonder Woman had Ares, Spiderman had the Green Goblin, and Batman had the Joker. Notice these are only one of the villains each superhero faced. The thing about villains is that when you defeat one, another is waiting in the wings. The same goes for the villainous words that we face in our life. You have multiple phrases and words waiting for you in the background of your life. When one is defeated, another pops up. The good news is, with every victory, you gain strength, knowledge, and wisdom to be better equipped to fight the next battle. Ask yourself, "What villains are you facing?"

What are the words destroying your self-esteem and eroding your confidence? What are the words playing repeatedly in your head when you start something new, trying to keep you the same? What are the words that undermine you? These words are the villains in your life.

Fear is a warning. It lets you know you are doing something and there is no guarantee of success. "You'll fail." "So many other people are doing the same thing, no one will even notice you." These words that induce fear in your life are villains to be fought. They seek out your weaker areas in life, searching for a way to destroy you, to hold you back or to make you content to live your live with your personal power negated.

Unlike the superheroes that choose to protect and hide their power until needed, villainous words try to keep you from understanding and believing you have powers in the first place. They want to take away your ability to fight and the will to be a superhero by causing you to believe you have nothing to fight for, with, or against. The goal of villainous words are to erode your identity and nullify your impact on the world around you. It has been said that graveyards are the richest places on the earth. They are filled with dreams unfulfilled, songs unwritten, stories untold, poems unspoken, lives unlived, emotions unsaid, potential unfulfilled and fears that ruled. Some of those lying there were superheroes who fought to overcome villains, others succumbed to the villainous words and left the richness of life without tasting the success that comes after the next battle.

The Words that Destroy and Suck Power from Your Life

Villainous words try to make you invisible wherever you go and ineffective even when you do act. They make you believe you are unheard when you do speak. They make you settle for the least you can do to get by, instead of striving for the best you can achieve throughout life. Words can create and destroy, there is both the power of life and death in them. Villainous words seek to destroy and cause death while you are living. This death is not always physical. It can be the death of dreams, ideas and even to confidence. Where in your life is death hiding or slowly encroaching? If you examine these areas in their entirety, you will find the villainous words present. They may have been there in the beginning, something you were unaware of in the moment. They could have crept in slowly throughout the course of a situation, slowing eating away at the foundations or structure being built. Or, they may have saved their final attack for the end, launching a full-scale battle out of nowhere.

One of the most powerful villains that I have faced in my adult life is that I am not good enough to help others because my own life is a mess. After I graduated from high school, I spent years in college trying to figure out what I wanted to do. I didn't have a clear plan going in and changed my major multiple times before settling on one long enough to graduate. As an introvert who is also self-contained, it was difficult for me to develop relationships with others because I was genuinely happier in my world of a few close friends, between the pages of a book, and the rich fantasy world in my mind. I was rarely bored and did not see the point of connecting with more people who would disrupt the life I was currently living. Conversations with strangers were fine because they fueled the stories in my mind, but the intentional development of a new connection took time and honestly, it was time I would rather spend on my own. The person may have been more than worth it, but I was too selfish to care.

On the other hand, I love to help people and see them succeed in their chosen fields. I am happy to help by being the person who researches a topic, asks questions, helps develop plans, takes notes and types them up for you. I am happy sitting in the room soaking up information as long as there is not a requirement for me to talk in front of too many people. So, I lived my life with the struggle of being self-contained and coming out of that containment to help others. Many times, self-containment won, and I would feel just bad enough that I would make a little more effort next time before I let self-containment win again. This was a recurring pattern in my life, and my relationships until a conversation with my best friend.

In this conversation she mentioned that I was a great friend, but it was hard to get to know me, especially in the initial stages of our friendship. It was a constant pulling of information and it took a lot of work to get to the point where she could see how good of a friend I could be. It hurt. The fact that I had asked a question, and this was her true answer did not negate the pain. Knowing there was no malice or desire to cause pain with the response didn't lessen the impact of the words in my soul. In fact, knowing they were the genuine response of someone very dear to me, spoke not out of anger or an attack against me as a person, but as a genuine evaluation of her truth spoken in love meant the words had a greater impact in me. The initial impact of pain was so profound, I sometimes feel the echoes of them today.

Yet, the pain of the situation elicited a question in my mind. Looking back on our friendship, could I see how she felt that way even if it was never my intention? Why did I not see it at the time and why were my actions what they were?

In my time of self-evaluation, I could see why she would think those things. It was difficult for me to open up to people and tell them what was on my mind because I always felt offbeat. I felt I was one step behind everyone else trying to figure out where to go and what to do. I didn't think I had much to contribute because others had their lives together and were working towards a goal. I was still trying to figure out if what I was working on today was the same thing as yesterday or if it somehow transformed while I was sleeping. This was even before thoughts of tomorrow came in.

I could listen to and talk about the goals of others because they were firm. I could research specific things, ideas and plans for them because it was concrete, but my life was in a state of flux. I didn't think sharing, "I don't know what I'm doing today" would make a difference. It would take further examination to realize these words playing my head went back to my third-grade teacher. "Kids go around thinking they're smart and can't even solve a basic math problem." Although I didn't consciously remember them, I could remember exactly how I felt and my body remembered walking away from the board, humiliated.

I had walked away with the words, "Don't show people how smart you are." Unknowingly, I had also walked away with the words, "Smart people don't know what they are doing." It was these unknown words that had become a major villain in my life. They had been working in the background of my life for over 15 years, so subtly I didn't even notice the erosion they were causing. Why would I help others and show them what was going on in my life when I didn't know what I was doing? When I had tried in the third grade, I was humiliated, embarrassed, talked about and not allowed to finish. I was living out my life in ways so I would not be put into that situation again.

Identifying some of the villainous words in your life may be easy. The ones you fight against the most easily come to mind because they are the ones you are most familiar with. However, there is also a set of villainous words that have lurked in the shadows of your life for so long you may not even think about them. They come out in actions and behaviors you have accepted are part of your personality. Having conversations with trusted people in your life and being willing to acknowledge their perspective without anger or hostility can begin the process of uncovering these hidden villains in your life.

Exercise

List the negative words you fight every day?

....
....
....
....
....
....
....
....
....

What are words that seem positive and cause a negative reaction within you? Why?

....
....
....
....
....
....
....
....
....

Look over the lists of major events in your life from the last chapter, the negative words you fight and the words that cause a negative reaction in you. Identify any themes or repeating words.

....
....
....
....
....
....
....
....
....

Make a list of situations in your life that are not ideal and areas that feel like they are dying.

....
....
....
....
....
....
....
....
....
....

The Words that Destroy and Suck Power from Your Life

What are the villainous words present in these situations?

....
....
....
....
....
....
....
....
....

Where did the words originate from and how do they impact the situation?

....
....
....
....
....
....
....
....
....

How were they instrumental to the destruction you see or how are they trying to destroy what you have?

....

....

....

....

....

....

....

How have they attacked? Do they come when you're starting something new? Do they come when you're relaxing, getting ready to sleep?

....

....

....

....

....

....

....

....

....

The Words that Destroy and Suck Power from Your Life

Which attacks have been successful or started to erode what was once stronger?

_____

_____

_____

_____

_____

_____

_____

_____

_____

Once you begin to examine these situations and notice how they have been active in your life, you can start to find your superpowers, the words that will help you fight against them.

CHAPTER 4:

SUPERPOWERS – THE STRENGTHS THAT WORDS HIDE OR REVEAL

In a world where phonebooths are rare and cameras monitor most of our lives, I wonder where Clark Kent would go to change. In a world where satellites cover the Earth, can the island of Themyscira stay hidden? In a place where the rich are constantly hounded by the paparazzi, could Bruce Wayne keep his secret identity a secret? In a city where people are apt to shoot first and ask questions later, would Spiderman still be alive after someone saw him climb a wall without footholds or a ladder? In a world where every part of a person's life can be subject to the critique of others, can we still harness the power of words? Some questions are not meant to be answered. They are simply asked to get you to *think*.

Superman's cape revealed to the world he was in superhero mode. Wonder Woman had her Lasso of Truth and bullet-stopping bracelets that marked her change. Iron Man became encased in a metal suit and Batman had a mask and utility belt. Each superhero had a signature weapon. Words are both the superpower and the tools that you use to fight your battles. Make them your signature weapon. Which words help you to reveal your strengths?

Before that question can be answered, you need to understand the functions of words.. Words can be used for a variety of things. They can be used to describe a personality trait, a characteristic, an action, or an emotion. They can also be used to attack a person's character, poke at weaknesses, scrape against insecurities, breakdown mental walls of protection, mock genuine attempts, or hinder emotional, mental, and spiritual growth. On the other hand, words can also build self-esteem, encourage through tough times, build up, celebrate achievements, or help you understand the world around you better.

Words used in one manner can induce tears and in another elicit laughter. They are versatile and depending on how and by who they are used, the same words put together in different formations can have extremely different results.

This is good news! It means for every set of words that have held you back, there is a set of words that will help propel you forward. For every word that has caused you to hide, there is a set of words that will help you reveal your true self. For every set of words that have eroded things in your life, there is a set of words that can rebuild areas of your life. For every word that has poked at a weakness, there is a word that can strengthen you. It's a relief to know that for everything words can destroy, by finding the right words to counteract them, bigger and better things can be built.

This is the strength of words that you can make your superpower. They can help you build your life bigger and better than you ever dreamed. Words never ask you to become someone different. Instead, with the proper application of words you become truer to who you are. You encourage strengths that have a chance to show greatness. You acknowledge areas of secondary strengths or weaknesses. Once acknowledged, you get to decide what to do about them. Do you continue trying to operate attempting to make these secondary strengths or weaknesses into primary strengths? Or do you use your words in your areas of primary strength until they become super?

Superman's weakness was Kryptonite. He could function for a time in the presence of this substance, but it weakened him. Could he have learned to function longer and better in its presence? After all, an entire race of people had lived on the planet before it was destroyed. There were generations of Kryptonians who thrived on the planet, living in the presence of the substance for generations without a problem. It was normal for his parents and any other person who had been born and grew up there. It was not a weakness for them.

But Kalel, or Clark, had been sent away so that his life would be saved. As a result, he was raised in a different environment. He grew up in the presence of a sun that strengthened his body, making him accustomed to the extra power it provided. He grew up learning to live with extra strength and power until it was his nature. A side effect was, in the presence of something that represented an absence of power it had the ability to weaken and even kill Superman.

Some people grow up through generations of words that no longer have an effect on them. It is commonplace. Yet, when you learn of a different environment, a set of words that strengthen you and you learn to live in the strength provided. Once the strength provided by words becomes a part of your nature, you can recognize when you are in the presence of words representing the absence of strength.

How do you find the strength? Ask yourself:

- What would I love?
- What are the things that you have hidden away in the deepest recesses of your mind that you would love, but life or people have made it seem impossible?
- What are the things you want to see, what are the aspects of the life you want to live?

Love strengthens. Peter Parker is an example of this. It was love for his uncle that induced Spiderman to fight. He fought first against the man who killed his uncle, but afterwards he began to fight for the city he lived in.

He heard the words of his uncle in his head. "With great power comes great responsibility." These are the words that strengthened him. In the same way, words can strengthen you. In moments of weakness, words spoken in love can sustain you, reframe situations, provide comfort, and let you know you are not alone. Words have the power to reach into your heart when you are struggling and help you to fight free.

Even science backs this. It lets us know that coma patients can hear words spoken to them. They may not be physically aware of what is going on, but words can penetrate the brain even when it's not conscious. Need a different example? Words can infiltrate your dreams.

Have you ever had a dream and woke up wondering what cause it? Later, you learn that you heard something on the radio or TV and it played a prominent role in your dream. This shows the power and functions of words. Words can seep into your subconscious, influence your dreams, speak to you in moments of deep physical stillness, and cut through mental anguish to reach the core of your identity. Once there, words can either reaffirm or subvert until you believe you are something that you are not. This is the power of words.

One thing can exponentially multiply the power of words in your life: Acceptance. What words do you accept over your life? Did you grow up hearing that children are to be seen and not heard? Did you accept it? Do you live your life with an underlying belief that your appearance is more important than what you say? Do you show up in life with a perfect outer appearance, but measure the words you say because you accepted showing up is acceptable, but telling your opinion or your story is not?

Did you grow up hearing money doesn't grow on trees? Do you move through life holding on to the majority of what you receive because you never know when you need it, and it's not readily available? Do you believe that you always have to strive for what you get and settle for wages far beneath your worth?

Did you grow up hearing, "You should be more like…" Fill in the blank. Do you go through life comparing yourself to others because your subconscious tells you every day you are not enough, and you should be more like …? Fill in the blank. Do you negate your own strengths because you see them as inferior to the strengths of others without recognizing that all strengths are needed, and your strength matches your personality?

Did you grow up hearing that you were stupid? Do you go through life ignoring the brilliant ideas and inventions that come to mind because you think everyone would laugh at you if they heard them because everyone knows that people don't listen to and laugh at stupid people?

Did you grow up hearing that failure is not an option? Do you go through life trying to be perfect without making mistakes? Are you afraid to learn new things because new things are learned through trial and error and you never want to hit the error stage?

Did you grow up hearing that you did a good job every time you tried something new? Do you go through life always willing to try regardless of the outcome because you did your best?

Did you grow up hearing you are a superstar? Do you go through life like all the world is your stage and as you give your best performance, people can't help by praise you?

Did you grow up hearing that you were smart? Do you walk into a room knowing that if you don't have the answer, you're smart enough to find the person who does?

Did you grow up hearing teamwork makes the dream work? Do you go through life searching for the best people to add to your team so your dreams will come through? Do you go through life looking for a team to be on so everyone can be successful?

Did you grow up hearing "You are smart. You are kind. You are important?" Do you go through life looking for opportunities to help or serve others? Do you look for ways to be kind to people every day? Do you rely on the strength and importance of who you are to make a positive difference in the lives of others?

What are the words in your life that give you strength? What are the words that propel you to be better and the words that you hold onto in the times of struggle? It is in these words your strengths are revealed. Even though you may know them instinctively, learning to identify them will help you to use them intentionally. Words used with intention can help you to feel your full strength. As your strengths are identified, you can leverage them to increase any area of your life until it reaches the level you want it to.

I am reminded of the movie *Inside Out*. In it, a family moved from their home because of the dad's job. The little girl tried to be happy and optimistic about leaving everything that she knew. She would act as though nothing was wrong even though she was slowing falling apart on the inside. Sadness was taking over her life, but she refused to let her parents see. She was struggling internally with words, or characters, that were out of place and unexpressed. It was destroying her and changing her personality. Eventually she tried to run away, to go back to the last place she was happy. Her parents caught her, and they finally set down to talk. It was only after she expressed the words fighting on the inside of her that she was able to move forward and build a bigger, better rounded, and more fleshed out personality. Attempting to hide from and not acknowledge the words that expressed emotion was slowly destroying her. When she expressed those words, she was able to find the right words that enabled her to grow.

As an internal processor, it is not always easy for me to talk through the process of what's happening in my mind. This was never more apparent than when I started teaching. I was a 7th grade mathematics instructor and trying to process the world along with everything else that goes on in the minds of students, with some of them barely able to speak English. I struggled a lot in my first year. I was part of a wonderful team and the other mathematics teachers were always willing to help, but in my classroom, it was just me and my students. I needed to find a way to teach them according to my strengths while working with their strengths on a timeline decided and set by the school district.

My progress was not measured wholly by what the students learned, but on how well they performed on a standardized test. It wasn't enough to have to deal with the parents, the school administration, and the district judging my teaching. I also had the added pressure of the state judging me based on the results of a test taken by students who may have test anxiety. It was a daily lesson in having stress piled on you and learning to manage it all.

My first step was to determine my strengths. My strengths lie in facilitating discussions, reading, listening, and asking questions. How was I supposed to use these strengths in a class of 7th graders while I was teaching math, a numbers subject? It took some time, but I came up with several ways to help me out. They included mathematical writing, projects, and having multiple other resources inside the classroom.

Giving students a prompt and having them write out how they would solve the problem let me see into their minds and get a better understanding of where they had trouble with concepts over calculations. Projects became sanity-savers for both me and the students. Students were more willing to listen and try to understand the lesson throughout the unit because they would have an opportunity to put it into action, not just take a test on it. By giving them a variety of representations to choose from, they could find something they liked to do.

Dislike ratios and proportions? It makes more sense when you get to design your dream home to scale and build a model. Don't understand the difference between perimeter, area and volume? Having the chance to build a cubic foot give you a physical representation. Having other resources in the classroom meant that I could spend more time walking around or working one-on-one with a student without others in the class getting restless because they were ready to move on. And taking a break so we could all go outside on a nice day was a way to change the environment, even if they had to write about what types of math they saw along the way.

These times did not make up the whole of the school year or eliminate all the stressors of teaching, but they did make life easier. Especially on a tough day, we could do something fun like color mandalas during a lesson on symmetry.

Many times, we hear about working on our weaknesses. This becomes a problem when we spend all our time working on our weakness and neglect the areas of strength. Working on a weakness may get you up to the level of competence. Working on a strength can make you a master.

Strengths are the areas in your life that *just make sense*. Some people can work in sales because they thrive off talking to people and are able to shake off a negative response without missing a step. Others can only hear "no" so many times before they are straddling the line into despair. Yet, they can look at a pile of data and pull out the relevant parts and organize it so that it makes sense.

Some people are good with numbers and can read through the books of a business while coming out with a smile. But the idea of them getting up on a stage in front of more than 20 people makes them sick to their stomach.

Should they work on public speaking? Maybe a little. However, if they can live their lives happily in numbers, teaching and helping others in small groups, writing books to explain the most common mistakes or concerns that they come across, they can become a leader in their field without ever having to step on a stage.

Knowing your strengths is an important part of being a superhero in your life. Superman can use his hands to stop a powerful locomotive. Spiderman trying to do the same thing will get him killed. He needs a different method to accomplish the same result. Learning your strengths and how to leverage them in life situations will help you to be the most powerful superhero you can be.

Exercise

Make a list of any words or phrases that came to your mind as you were going through this chapter.

....
....
....
....
....
....
....
....

Look back over your previous lists and determine what function the words had in your life.

Separate your lists into words that helped you and words that hindered you in some way.

....
....
....
....
....
....
....
....

How did some words help and how did some words hinder?

What actions do you still take today because of these words?

The Strengths That Words Hide or Reveal

On another sheet of paper, list out the areas of success and struggle in your life. Place the words that affect that area under the appropriate sections. Do this for both words that help and words that hinder. What do you notice?

Make a list of the strengths that come to light. Are there any strengths that show up that you didn't recognize before?

....
....
....
....
....
....
....
....

What are the words that can help you to leverage these strengths in the best way possible?

....
....
....
....
....
....
....
....

Take the time to look up quotes or books about the strengths you discovered. Write down the quotes that resonate with you.

....
....
....
....
....
....
....
....
....

Make a note of the books you may want to read or listen to later. Knowing your strengths is a great start. Learning more about them will help you to master and leverage them so they can provide the most benefit in your life.

Now that you have begun to understand the functions of words as both villains and superpowers, it's time to put them to use in your life and develop your plan of attack.

CHAPTER 5:

PLAN OF ATTACK

Have you ever rehearsed something in your mind so many times it feels like it took place in real life? Have you ever been on autopilot throughout the day and ending up at a destination without remembering the journey? Have you ever planned an event, going over every detail so meticulously that you are ready for every eventuality?

The process may be stressful, but at the end, there is peace in the fact that you have an answer for almost anything that could happen. The same thing applies with words. By now, you have developed a list of the words that you hear regularly in life. You have noted some common themes, your reactions to them and when they occur. The next step is to create a plan of attack you can use when these words come against you. By knowing the most frequent words you will battle, you can have a plan of attack already in place.

Words have different functions. They can encourage and belittle. They can praise or criticize. They can express love or hatred. They can build up or tear down. Some words cause us to think, some we instinctively reject. Some we ponder because the phrasing leaves us confused and some words, we hold in reserve for just the right moment. Creating a plan of attack means finding words that can be held in reserve, so we know what to say when the villains come around. Every time we hear a negative word or something that pokes at our weakness, we can have a response ready and waiting. Iron Man practiced with his blasters, Wonder Woman had her lasso of truth, Spiderman has his webs, and you can use your words.

What about the words that get past us or the moments when we are so used to the way things are, we don't realize it is a moment of attack? That's where our training and conditioning kick in, but that's for a later chapter.

Having a plan of attack simply means knowing what you are going to do when a certain situation happens. If someone tells you that you're ugly, do you accept it? Or do you say, "No I'm not. I am gorgeous. External beauty fades, the beauty I have will continue to grow."

If someone tells you that you are worthless, how do you respond? Do you walk away feeling like they are right, or do you recognize you have value on multiple levels? First, for being a living human being and then for every aspect of your personality.

When you hear the words that imply you are stupid or damaged, do you shrug and go along with it? Or do you tell yourself that although your strengths are not recognized by them or mainstream society, it doesn't negate or lessen them.

These are the questions that will help you develop your plan of attack. What words do you hear that cause a negative reaction within you? What will you do about it?

This is just one way that an attack can come. You can see these coming because it's usually the same people. It's similar to a punch in the face. It hurts and has the ability to knock you flat on your back. There are other attacks that come from behind, hitting you in the back of the knees to make you stumble or fall. Then there are words that come from below your level of awareness, catching you off guard and snapping your head back. At times, it may be a wall of words coming towards you all at the same time with the force of a blast.

With advanced planning, you can fight back against them all. Sometimes, you build up so many positive words within you that it blocks the negative ones coming at you. Sometimes, they need to be dodged or avoided. Yet others need a counterattack in order to defeat them and rob them of their strength. There is a science and an art to fighting that can be used when developing a plan of attack.

One approach is to counter strength with wisdom. What are the areas of your own strength and knowledge? How can you use these areas against the strength of negative words? If your strength is in words, write out the words you can use and keep them on hand. If your strength is in speaking, say the words out loud to yourself every day and especially when you feel an attack. If your strength is in action, purposefully do something that proves counter to the words that come against you. If your strength is in music, compose and sing a song that rebuts the words coming against you. If your strength is in art, sketch, draw, or build something that uplifts and strengthens you. If your strength is in nature, surround yourself by pieces of it and use the analogies that come to mind in order to face what is thrown at you. One example is to see yourself standing tall and rooted as a tree, facing the storm of words. You have enough flexibility to sway and not break, but you are grounded enough to still be standing when it is over.

There are many ways you can be attacked but having a plan in place can help you feel more prepared.

When you are facing a wall of words that come at you like a blast, you may need help from trusted people in your life. As you stand firm and fight back, your words along with the words of others fighting on your side and strengthening you with positive words and actions can help make a difference.

Look for these people in your life and ask for their help. You can ask in the moment you need or beforehand. Knowing the people in your life you can count on to help will give your mind a sense of ease. Knowing that you are not alone lets you focus on cultivating and building yourself up with the assurance someone has your back during moments of weakness.

I am fortunate to have a great family, but I truly began to understand the importance of this when I met my best friend. We did not start out that way, but I know that I can always count on her. Within the first year of us meeting, I had a life situation that knocked me off my feet. I felt like everyone had abandoned me and people in my life that I thought would love me, turned their back on me. I was devastated along with being separated from my family and any source of support. I was on my own living a life that didn't stop or slow down because my world was reeling. I needed a safe place badly while I tried to shore up the sides of a life that crumbled before I could even get to it.

Then there was this girl who people were telling me wanted to fight me over an ex-boyfriend. Unbeknownst to me, they were telling her the same thing. In a world that was already crumbling and adrift, I couldn't handle this additional stress, so we had a conversation. We found out we were both being lied to and began a tentative friendship that has grown to become one of the foundational relationships in my life.

We spent much of the first couple months in each other's presence in silence. It was a silence without pressure and judgement. A silence where I could build without being attacked. A silence, that even when broken required no more than I could handle. It was in this silence that I was able to rebuild walls that words had decimated and with this support that I found the courage to plan and fight back.

It was many years before I could tell her how much those early months of friendship meant to me. The silent support of a friend through a devasting time in my life. She never pressed and eventually I was able to explain what I had been dealing with throughout that time. This is a relationship that I can count on to always have my back, provide strength in weak moments and help when needed. Each day, I pray I can provide the same to her.

Sometimes, when you are facing a wall of words as an attack, the best plan is to find a place where you can shelter down until it has passed. Having a place where you can sit out the storm and take inventory of the damage done is essential. Sometimes, the right words will not come to you until you know exactly what they destroyed.

Developing a plan of attack includes a multitude of situations. It will help you prepare for the battle of words you face going through life. Knowing what words, types of words, or themes that affect you the most will give you an opportunity to combat them.

Exercise

Look at each of the words and phrases that you've written down on your negatives list. Come up with a rebuttal for each one. Asking people you trust can help you see yourself from a different perspective. They can even help you with words, but write in your own words. It will have more power if you choose the words then if you use someone else's words.

....
....
....
....
....
....
....

Look at each of the words and phrases on your positives list. How can you put these into action for you every day?

....
....
....
....
....
....
....
....

Plan of Attack

Write down your strengths. What do you come back to on a regular basis during emotional highs and lows in your life? What helps you to make it through the day?

....
....
....
....
....
....
....
....
....
....
....

How can you use these strengths in your plan of attack?

....
....
....
....
....
....
....
....
....
....

There will always be sneak attacks, things you can't plan for because you never saw them coming. If this happens to you, don't be surprised. Add it to your plan of attack so you are ready the next time.

Being prepared for the battle will help relieve stress and provide peace day to day. Your brain has something positive to focus on and can be working to strengthen you. While a plan of what to do when something happens is helpful, it can be strengthened by the daily training and conditioning plan you have in place. Your conditioning will also kick in to help you when sneak attacks come.

CHAPTER 6:

TRAINING PLAN – CONDITIONING YOURSELF FOR SUCCESS

The Karate Kid, while a good movie, would not make the list of my top ten favorite films. I tend to enjoy more Disney movies. But even years after watching it, I remember the scenes of wax on, wax off and paint the fence. I also remember the kick at the end and have tried to do it many times. Yet it was the fact the seemingly everyday tasks can be used to train and condition the muscles for movements that can be used in karate that stuck with me.

Watching scenes of Spiderman trying and failing to move from building to building using his webs, Superman learning to adjust his power and Ironman learning to use his suit properly so that he doesn't end up crashing into a wall just reinforced this fact. Training was necessary in order to have the maximum effectiveness in what they did and to become better at what they wanted to do.

They spent weeks and months trying, failing, learning, and improving. This is the same thing we must do. Practice makes perfect is a saying that you hear often, or rather perfect practice makes perfect. We work to find what is most effective for us and practice it. We learn from the mistakes and failures to refine our plans and continue working until we have a plan that is right for us. We condition ourselves daily and train until the motions and movements become automatic. Then periodically, we review with intention and adjust based off our current situations and level. It's how we build up our inherent power, so we are ready for the next attack.

Most athletes have a strict training routine. If you were an athlete, you remember the time spent in drills. If you're not, you may have heard about them, seen them on tv or read about them in a book. The repetitive practice over and over so that in the heat of the moment, responses become engrained and automatic. Life is the same way. There are responses and reactions that have been conditioned into us and when we began to fight for a better or different life, we may need to change the way we were previously conditioned.

But how? This is where a training plan comes into play. It will help us so that in the midst of the action or circumstance, our response and reaction will be automatic. Wouldn't it be great if every time you heard the words, "You're stupid," your brain would automatically reply, "No! You're not." Tell yourself, "I was born smart and continue to be. I may not know as much as you in this area, but I am capable of learning it." The true question is" Do you want to know more about this or are you content with your current knowledge in this field because you're choosing to be more knowledgeable in another.

I know that was a long answer, but it doesn't always have to be. It only needs to be an answer to combat the villainous words you faced in a way that resonates with you.

Where do we start in developing a training plan? Start with your values. What are the core aspects of what you believe about life and people? What things are essential to the way you view the world and who you want to be?

Then, research or talk to people who have been successful in or are doing what you want to do. Find out the things they are saying and doing regularly. Try this out for at least a month to see what works for you.

There is no right answer. Some people use scriptures, affirmations, others use meditation, some use a think this, not that type of method. For others, speaking out loud works for them, making personal movies, listening to motivational speaking and podcasts or journals are just some tips that you can find online. Find the ones that work for you.

How? Pick one and try it out. Try it for about a month as listed, then adjust as needed to continue for another month. After the month is over, reflect on your experiences. Do you feel worse? What do you need to change? Make the changes and try it for another month, reflect.

If it is something that you absolutely hate and you cringe every single time or if it makes you miserable, stop. Try something different.

Notice, in your reflection, you evaluate for if you feel worse. Some people may see positive results right away.

Yay! Congratulations!

For other people, it will take time to change the way their life is going and looking for immediate change will only increase disappointment. It will also allow those villainous words a chance to make another appearance. Other times, we cannot see the change happening in our life because it is a gradual process.

Have you ever tried to gain weight or release it? Other people notice before you do, because we are constantly with ourselves and the brain adapts to the little changes that happen. When we see others, they may have a frozen picture of us in their minds from the last time they saw us. If they don't see us every day, they notice quicker the difference between the picture in their mind and the reality in front of them.

If you look for immediate positive change, you may be disappointed. Looking to see if anything is worse, allows time for reflection over both the actions and words that you have been saying, but also over the quality of your life. You may still be working in the same place, but you may not be as drained at the end of the day. You may have noticed that the antics of your coworkers is the same, but you have started to take the time to understand them. Or, you may have begun to put a plan in place to move on. If you look only for positive change, you may stop at the fact that you are in the same job. When you switch to reflection in order to see if anything is worse, you will start to see little changes indicating your superpower is emerging.

If something is causing you harm, stop. If it's a little uncomfortable, but there is no harm being done, continue a little longer. Things may be working for you and it's taking time for you to see the change because it's starting at a deeper point in your life than you are consciously aware.

After the second month, take a break for a day or two. If you continue with your conditioning plan automatically, that's fine. Just don't intentionally do it. What do you notice? Is everything working for you? Do you need to make modifications? Is there an aspect that you want to throw out and move on to the next item on your list?

Training using words can start with lists. You have created lists of words that cause a negative and a positive reaction in your life that you hear on a regular basis. You are aware of the ones that are used most often and the ones that have the greatest impact on you. This is your starting list.

Take a look at the negative words you hear most often, the ones that create the most negative reaction within you and the words that impact you the most in a negative manner. Are they true? Take the top five and write down the circumstances where you first remember hearing them. What was going on that caused the words to be said? What were you doing and how were you feeling? Now, know that you know about the whole situation, are the words true? What are other words that could have been said in that situation?

Dealing with money was not an area of great strength for me. Now, I can budget, pay my bills on time, invest along with setting up and contributing to a savings account. I have an idea of how much money I have in the bank and I check my account regularly. I thrive with the ability to know how to do tasks that a lot of people cannot manage. At one time, I was included in that group.

I am proud of where I am, but at times I have to unsubscribe from newsletters or emails because they talk about where I should be based off of what I should have done. I can do this with confidence because I have specific words in my mind. I may not have done what you thought I should have done at a time when you think, but I am in a good place now. I know and can get help from people that meet me where I am and use their expertise to show me where I can go, not where I should have been. I have conditioned myself to this response when I come across something that brings us my previous lack of skill instead of encouraging me where I am.

Yet, this skill was not learned overnight and for a long time I felt bad that dealing with money was not a strength. I could manage to eventually pay my bills and everything else, but I was always playing catch up. I learned to use the tools available to help me set a budget, track my expenses, even track my investing. But I had to let go of the words telling me I had to do everything myself and I needed to know absolutely everything about my money, or I was setting myself up for failure.

The first time I remember being told I was bad with money I was a child. While the age eludes me, the circumstances do not. I lost $20. It was there one minute and then it was gone. I had it in the bathroom, thought I put it down to wash my hands, and walked out. When I went back to look for it, it was gone. I told my parents what happened, and they asked, "How could you lose $20?" I didn't know, it just disappeared.

Looking back on this situation, I can see it a little differently. Was I bad with money? No. I was careless in that given situation. I was forgetful. I should have been more conscientious, but I wasn't bad with money.

I have often left things in the bathroom because I needed to wash my hands and they were still there when I went back for them. As part of my training plan, I made myself take an extra step to look around the bathroom after I wash my hands to ensure nothing was left behind. On a second scan, I often see things that I would have previously needed to return for. I wasn't bad with money. I was careless in a situation and because of conditioning, I was able to help negate that area of forgetfulness.

Another area of conditioning for me involves writing. When I decided to write a book, I started out with research because I am a researcher at heart. An Internet search will bring up multiple lists and advice about what works and what does not. Some tell you to write first thing in the morning, others say write when it works best for you. There are also different time periods listed. Times range from 15 minutes to one hour. All this conflicting advice can make your head spin. So, I looked for the similarities, the things that tended to work for most people. I found two. Making time to write needed to be intentional and it needed to be on a regular basis.

I then spoke with a writer friend of mine. Her advice was to sit down in front of the computer and write without worrying about the quality. So, this is where I started. I picked a time and sat in front of the computer to write. I had a time frame and sat down for an hour every day.

It was not feasible for me. I struggled to do every day, but I could manage four to five days a week. My starting time changed based on life, yet usually within a couple of hours of waking up, I pull out my laptop, sit on my floor and pull up my writing. Some days, I write more than others. Some days, as soon as the screen comes up, words come to my mind. Other days, it takes longer. But I sit for my allotted time that day in front of the computer.

Some days, I am amazed and other days I cringe. Yet, I have trained myself to sit and write. I can always hire an editor to help make it all fit together coherently, but they can't help me if I never have any words to give them.

Exercise

Part of increasing fitness is pushing your body to be uncomfortable and adapting to a new level. This is the same principle applied when you are working on word fitness.

Look at your lists of positive words and of rebuttals. Start to say them out loud. At first, it may be uncomfortable, or you may not believe them. Write down your first reactions to them.

....
....
....
....
....
....
....

Stay consistent for a month and give your brain time to adjust. What reactions do you have now?

....
....
....
....
....
....
....

If the new words are completely wrong for you, adjust them until they fit. If they are a little uncomfortable, but something that you can handle, keep going. Say them out loud and mentally to yourself. Let your brain mull over them while you are going throughout your day. Say them the next day and the next letting the process continue. Before long, you may find yourself seeing areas in your life where those words are true.

While the words you tell yourself can change overnight, it doesn't mean the words you're previously told yourself will disappear as quickly. This is where your training plan comes into play. Train your mind in the new words that you want to say to yourself. Train your mouth to speak and respond in new ways.

Daily training and conditioning will increase the likelihood of you responding in new ways until one day you look back and realize it has become automatic. What are you making a part of your daily routine that will help you in the long run?

This routine will change and adjust as you change. Give yourself grace to make adjustments and to not get it right every time. When you reflect over your day, you may be surprised by what helps and what hinders you. These adjustments you make will solidify over time to a personal routine that helps you live your best life. Your new way of thinking, enhanced by the daily conditioning and routines will help you to show up daily as your authentic self.

CHAPTER 7:
YOUR AUTHENTIC SELF

Look at how far you've come. You've taken the time to identify the words in your life that have played a major role in where you are now. This includes both the positive words and the words that have held you back. You know the identity that you have chosen to accept. The choice is yours. Many times, we feel forced into a role by the words spoken to or about us by others. We have accepted the words of others and allowed them to hold sway in our lives to the point where we either use those words as a chance to excel or as a reason to not fully live. When you identify the words surrounding your life now and the words needed for you to live your best life, you began to see the existing disparities and make a choice on how to handle them.

When looking back on your life, it is sometimes the easiest and most natural thing to identify the negative things. Identifying the positive things can be challenging and takes practice. But good can also be found. That good is attached to the words that cause a positive reaction in us. We fight with the good words in our lives. We cling to them as they have developed and defined our strengths. We know what we are good at usually because someone has pointed it out to us or praised us for it. We may have told ourselves after many challenges that we are going to be better. Speaking repeatedly to ourselves, we learn more, take risks and live our lives. Looking back, we can begin to see that the words continually spoken to ourselves turned into a superpower in our lives. Using these words intentionally, help us to uncover our strengths and find our superpower. They make us feel strong for the challenges we face knowing that we will come out victorious.

Knowing the superheroes in our lives balance learning about the villainous words. Often, we see the bad, but struggle to understand where it came from. Acknowledging that the villainous words in our lives are often the cause of negative things that we see in our lives gives us a starting point. Words spoken to us when we were younger, were accepted and internalized. As a result, we live our lives on autopilot to avoid feeling like we did in those moments. Those words, villains, so engrained in our life hold us back without conscious acknowledgment. Identifying these types of villainous words come through conversations with others that we both trust to be honest with us and whose perspectives we choose to accept.

Identifying the subtle villainous words in our life can often help us to realize why we fight so often against the blatant villainous words in our lives. By identifying them both, we know exactly what battles we will face every day and we can choose if and how we will fight.

Once you are aware of the words that empower you and the words that drain you, you are in the position to find words whose powers you can use to change your life. You can read scriptures, find quotes, use affirmations, or create your own series of words that you choose to have power in your life.

Regardless of the source, make them work for you. It does you no good if you only recite words from memory that do not resonate with you.

Starting off, you may not completely believe the words you say and that's okay. The question at that point is, "Do these words resonate with you in a positive way? Is it something that you want to work towards? Is it something you can leverage to be stronger, go further and increase your world?" These are the important factors, and it is in these emotions within yourself that the power of words become superpowers you can wield.

After you have your superpower words, it is time to put them to work for you. Let's make a plan. Just as a fighter would be unprepared if they tried to counter a punch using a move designed to counter a kick, our best efforts fall short if we are using our words in an inappropriate context.

We need to know what our words are combatting so we use them in the best situations. Using words that encourage us to push harder during a physical challenge against an attack on our character may help, but it is inefficient. When our character is attacked, using words designed to strengthen our knowledge of our identity and the way we show up every day will be most effective. We use a counter to a punch when a punch is thrown.

Using words that strengthen us when we work towards excellence against an attack on our work ethic has the best chance to both neutralize the attack towards us and strengthen us at the same time. Learning to use words efficiently has this dual power. They strengthen us while they fight against and weaken the villains that come against us.

After having our superpowers and a plan of attack, conditioning comes in. It's great to know what to do when an attack comes. Conditioning helps build our strength ahead of time. We can safeguard the areas where we are already strong and build up the areas where we are weak. Building up areas of weaknesses in our lives doesn't negate the pain. It does mean that it may hurt less. Conditioning our self also means there may come a time when we learn to react automatically. Our word muscle memory is activated, and we can block some of the sneak attacks that take place because our brains are conditioned to look out for them and respond. They will still be unwelcome, but we learn to respond with ease.

It is after we put all these components in place that we can live confident of the battles that are ahead. With each step, we learn more about our self, our character, our strengths, our weaknesses, the words that strengthen us, those that weaken us and the ones we can use as superpowers to fight. Being able to fully utilize and overcome battles of negative words from others and negative words we tell ourselves open the pathway for us to walk through life authentically. We live authentic to who we are and create the life we want to live.

You are a superhero in your own right. You can impact and change the world, right where you are. More importantly, you can change your own life. Words are the superpower that will get you on your way. Learn the words that have the most power in your life and use them, wisely, every day. Condition your mind, build up your strength against the villainous words that come against you and fight back with the words that impact you and are on your side to change your life. For this is your unique superpower.

So, decide on your superhero name. Will you put on a cape, take off your glasses and enter the world as Superman? Or will you put on glasses and work as a reporter, understanding the power of words in your daily life as Clark Kent?

Will you put on a mask and fill up your belt with gear, driving out in the Batmobile while showing up daily as Batman? Or will you walk boldly into the power you were born with as Bruce Wayne?

Will you live as an Amazonian princess, ruling her island and raising future generations to understand the power they have as Princess Diana of Themyscira? Or will you choose to leave your place of origins and join others to help them fight their battles as Wonder Woman?

Will you live your life content to make it through the day helping those close to you like Peter Parker? Or will you use what you have learned and what was given to you by an accident to make the world a little safer like Spiderman?

The answer lies with you and the words you choose each day as your superpower. Now that you are aware of the words you speak, and the ones you accept, you have a choice to make. Will you choose words that empower you or words that weaken you?

With every word or phrase spoken about you, you have a decision to make. Will you accept the villainous words, or will you use your own superpower to fight back in the battles and skirmishes you face every day, eventually emerging victorious? What is your alter ego and what is your authentic self? Will you have the strength and confidence to live true to yourself?

Will you train and condition yourself daily so you are ready for and can face regular attacks with ease?

Only you can answer theses questions. Only you can make the decision to change.

CONCLUSION

You've done it. You've identified the negative words holding you back, those you face on a regular basis from others, and even those you face on a regular basis from yourself. It's a thorough process and at times tough.

You've also identified positive words impacting your life, developed a training plan and a daily routine to build consistency and strength. I am so proud of you. You now have everything you need to make words your superpower every day.

Now, live! Don't forget to review periodically. As you get stronger, you will need to adjust your training routine. New words may be used against you. Knowing and preparing for what may come is half the battle.

Superman lived as Clark Kent until it was time for him to step fully into who he was. Batman lived as Bruce Wayne until he was needed more and more. Spiderman lived his life fully confident in his powers even throughout the day as Peter Parker. Now that you have your superpower within you, you can do the same.

There is no need to hide behind negative words, thinking that you can't do anything or that you are not good enough. You know that you are. It doesn't matter if you are a super teacher, super accountant, super CEO, super maintenance technician, or a super "enter your title here," you have the knowledge to use words to be the best version of yourself. Your actions will align with the new words you speak to yourself.

www.ingramcontent.com/pod-product-compliance
Lightning Source LLC
Chambersburg PA
CBHW020913080526
44589CB00011B/580